# Foundations in Accountancy / ACCA

# Financial Accounting (FFA/FA)

First edition 2011, Seventh edition January 2018

ISBN 9781 5097 1746 0

eISBN 9781 5097 1895 5

**British Library Cataloguing-in-Publication Data**

A catalogue record for this book is available from the
British Library

Published by

BPP Learning Media Ltd
BPP House, Aldine Place
142–144 Uxbridge Road
London W12 8AA

www.bpp.com/learningmedia

Printed in the United Kingdom

Your learning materials, published by BPP Learning
Media Ltd, are printed on paper obtained from traceable
sustainable sources.

Welcome to BPP Learning Media's **Foundations in Accountancy / ACCA Financial Accounting (FFA/FA) Passcards.**

- They **focus on your exam** and **save you time.**

- They incorporate **diagrams** to kick start your memory.

- They follow the overall **structure** of the BPP Interactive Texts, but BPP Learning Media's new **Passcards** are not just a condensed book. Each card has been separately designed for clear presentation. Topics are self contained and can be grasped visually.

- **Passcards** are still **just the right size** for pockets, briefcases and bags.

Run through the **Passcards** as often as you can during your final revision period. The day before the exam, try to go through the **Passcards** again! You will then be well on your way to passing your exams.

### Good luck!

For reference to the Bibliography of the Foundations in Accountancy / ACCA Financial Accounting (FFA/FA) Passcards please go to: www.bpp.com/learning-media/about/bibliographies

## Contents

**Page**

# 1: Introduction to accounting

## Topic List

The purpose of financial reporting

Types of business entity

Users

Governance

The main financial statements

*This chapter looks at why financial statements are prepared, the different types of business entities and the users of financial statements.*

*We also look at the main financial statements: the statement of financial position and the statement of profit or loss.*

## The purpose of financial reporting

Financial reporting enables businesses to record, analyse and summarise financial data.

A business has a number of functions, the most prominent is to make a profit for the owners

**Profit is the excess of income over expenditure**

## Types of business entity

Sole traders – Refers to ownership, sole traders can have employees

Partnerships – Two or more people working together to earn profits

⎱ Personally responsible for debts of business

Limited liability company – Owners have liability limited to the amount they pay for their shares

– A limited liability company has a separate legal identity from its owners

### Users of financial statements

- Managers of the company
- Shareholders of the company
- Trade contacts
- Providers of finance to the company
- Taxation authorities
- Employees of the company
- Financial analysts and advisors
- Government and their agencies
- The public

The larger the entity, the greater the interest from various groups of people.

Different users have different needs.

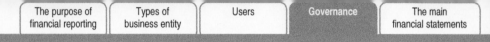

## Governance

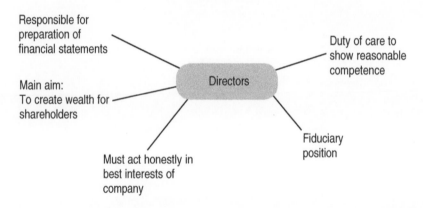

Responsible for preparation of financial statements

Main aim:
To create wealth for shareholders

Directors

Duty of care to show reasonable competence

Fiduciary position

Must act honestly in best interests of company

## Main financial statements

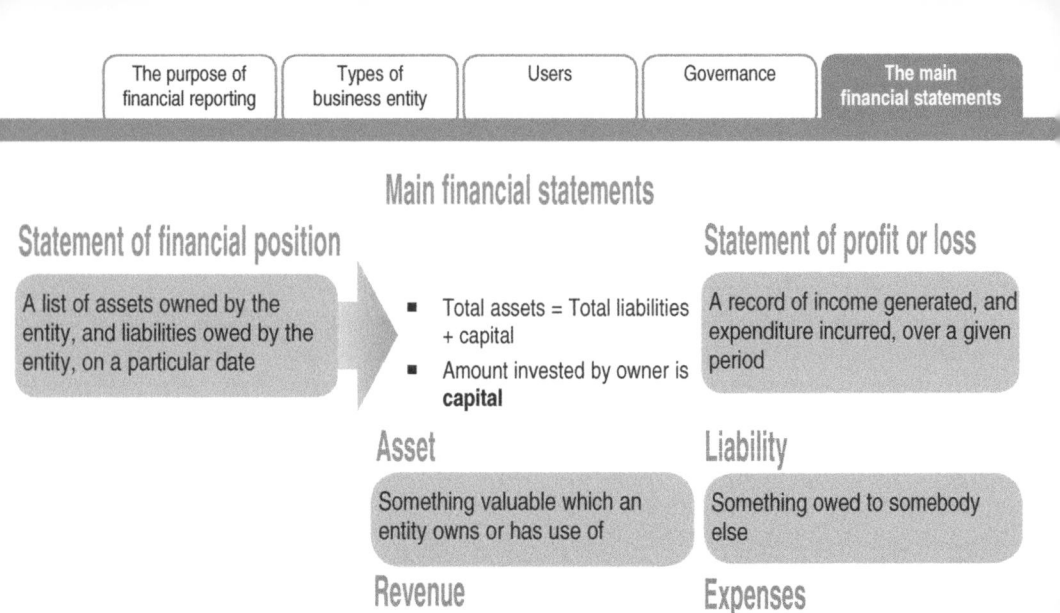

### Statement of financial position

A list of assets owned by the entity, and liabilities owed by the entity, on a particular date

- Total assets = Total liabilities + capital
- Amount invested by owner is **capital**

### Statement of profit or loss

A record of income generated, and expenditure incurred, over a given period

### Asset

Something valuable which an entity owns or has use of

### Liability

Something owed to somebody else

### Revenue

Income generated by a business

### Expenses

Costs of running a business

# 2: The regulatory framework

## Topic List

The regulatory system

IASB

International Financial Reporting Standards (IFRSs)

*This chapter looks at the regulatory system and the role played by the IASB.*

## National law

Form and content of accounts may be regulated by national legislation.

## Accounting standards

The IASB produces International Financial Reporting Standards (IFRSs).

## Influences upon financial accounting

## Other requirements

Drawn from:

- Statutory requirement in other countries
- Stock exchanges

## Accounting concepts and individual judgement

Can lead to subjectivity. Accounting standards were developed to address subjectivity.

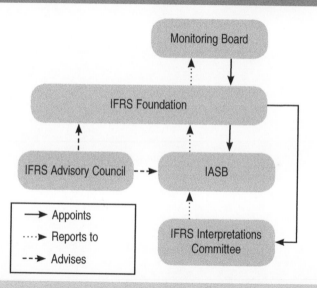

## Objectives of IFRS Foundation are to:

1) Develop a single set of high quality, understandable, enforceable and globally accepted IFRSs through standard-setting body IASB
2) Promote use and rigorous application of these standards
3) Take account of the needs of emerging economies and SMEs
4) Bring about convergence of national accounting standards and IFRSs to high quality solutions

## The use and application of IFRSs

IFRSs have helped to improve and harmonise financial reporting around the world. The standards are used in the following ways:

- As national requirements
- As the basis for all or some national requirements
- As an international benchmark for those countries which develop their own requirements
- By regulatory authorities for domestic and foreign companies
- By companies themselves

Notes

# 3: The qualitative characteristics of financial information

## Topic List

The IASB's *Conceptual Framework*

*Financial accounting is based on certain concepts and conventions.*

*Get to grips with these and you should be well equipped to discuss accounting standards and their strengths and weaknesses.*

### Going concern

The entity will continue in operation for the foreseeable future. There is no intention to put the entity into liquidation.

Underlying assumption

### Accruals

Revenue and costs must be recognised as they are earned or incurred, not as money is received or paid.

Not an underlying assumption, but accounts should be prepared on an accruals or matching basis.

# Qualitative characteristics

***Conceptual Framework*** ⟶ Qualitative characteristics make information in financial statements useful to users.

## Two fundamental characteristics

- Relevance
- Faithful representation

**Relevance** — Information is relevant when it influences decisions of users, affected by nature and materiality

**Materiality**
Information is material if its omission or misstatement could influence the economic decisions of users taken on the basis of the financial statements

**Faithful representation** — Financial information must faithfully represent the underlying economic phenomena

— Complete, neutral, free from error

## Enhancing characteristics:

**Comparability**
- Users must be able to compare financial statements through time and with other entities
- Disclose accounting policies
- Disclose corresponding info for comparative periods

**Verifiability**
- Information that can be independently verified

**Timeliness**
- Information is available in time to be capable of influencing decisions

**Understandability**
- Users must be able to understand financial statements
- Users assumed to have reasonable knowledge of business and economic activities
- Complex matters should not be left out if relevant

Other concepts

### Business entity concept

- In accounting, the business is treated as separate to its owners.

  **Not** the same as limited liability!

### Fair presentation

- Financial statements are required to present fairly in all material respects the financial results and position of the business.

  Compliance with IFRSs will achieve this.

### Consistency

- Presentation and classification of items should remain consistent from one period to the next, except if there is a change in operations or a change is required by IFRS.

# 4: Sources, records and books of prime entry

## Topic List

The role of source documents

Sales and purchase day books

Cash books

*This chapter covers the main sources of data and the function each source document or record has.*

*We will see how the documents are recorded in books of prime entry to reflect business transactions.*

## Source documents

Business transactions are nearly always recorded on a document. These documents are the source of the information in the accounts. Such documents include the following:

- Invoice
- Credit note
- Debit note
- Goods received note
- Goods despatch note
- Receipt

## Books of prime entry

The source documents are recorded in books of prime entry including the sales day book, purchase day book, and cash book.

## Journal

Journals are used to record source information that is not contained within the other books of prime entry. They record the following:

- Period end adjustments
- Correction of errors
- Large/unusual transactions

# Sales day book

The sales day book is used to keep a list of all invoices sent out to credit customers each day. Here is an example.

## SALES DAY BOOK

| Date | Invoice number | Customer | Rec'bles ledger ref. | Total invoiced $ |
|------|------|------|------|------|
| 3.3.X9 | 207 | ABC & Co | SL12 | 4,000 |
| | 208 | XYZ Co | SL59 | 1,200 |
| | | | | 5,200 |

# Purchase day book

This is used to keep a record of invoices which a business receives for credit purchases. Here is an example.

## PURCHASE DAY BOOK

| Date | Supplier | Payables ledger ref. | Total invoiced $ |
|------|------|------|------|
| 3.4.X9 | RST Co | PL31 | 215 |
| 10.4.X9 | JMU Inc | PL19 | 1,804 |
| 15.4.X9 | DDT & Co | PL24 | 758 |
| | | | 2,777 |

4: Sources, records and books of prime entry

## Cash book

Cash receipts and payments are recorded in the cash book.

Cash receipts are recorded as follows, with the total column analysed into its component parts.

### CASH RECEIPTS

| Date | Narrative | Total $ | Rec'bles ledger $ | Cash sales $ | Sundry $ |
|------|-----------|---------|-------------------|--------------|----------|
| 3.3.X9 | Cash sale | 150 | | 150 | |
| | Receivable: | | | | |
| | ABC & Co | 1,000 | 1,000 | | |
| | | 1,150 | 1,000 | 150 | – |

Cash payments are recorded in a similar way.

# Petty cash book

Petty cash payments and receipts are recorded in a petty cash book. Under the imprest system, the amount of money in petty cash is kept at an agreed sum or 'float', (say $50).

> Most businesses keep a small amount of cash on the premises for small payments, eg stamps, coffee.
>
> ## PETTY CASH BOOK
>
> | | RECEIPTS | | | | PAYMENTS | | | | |
> |---|---|---|---|---|---|---|---|---|---|
> | Date | Narrative | Total | Date | Narrative | Total | | Stationery | Coffee | etc |
> | | | $ | | | $ | | $ | $ | $ |
> | 3.3.X9 | Bank | 50 | 3.3.X9 | Paper | 10 | | 10 | | |
> | | | — | | Coffee | 5 | | — | 5 | |
> | | | 50 | | | 15 | | 10 | 5 | |

## Petty cash imprest system

Under the imprest system:

|  | $ |
|---|---|
| Cash still held in petty cash | 35 |
| Plus voucher payments | 15 |
| Must equal the agreed sum or float | 50 |

Reimbursement is made equal to the voucher payments to bring the float back up to the imprest amount.

# 5: Ledger accounts and double entry

## Topic List

The nominal ledger

The accounting equation

Double entry bookkeeping

The journal

Day book analysis

The receivables and payables ledgers

*This chapter looks at ledger accounting.*

*Ledger accounts summarise all the individual transactions listed in the books of prime entry.*

## Ledger accounting and double entry

Method used to summarise transactions in the books of prime entry.

A ledger account or 'T' account looks like this.

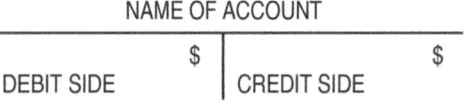

NAME OF ACCOUNT

|  | $ |  | $ |
| DEBIT SIDE | | CREDIT SIDE | |

## The nominal ledger

Is an accounting record which summarises the financial affairs of a business.

Accounts within the nominal ledger include the following:

- Plant and machinery (non-current asset)
- Inventories (current asset)
- Sales (income)
- Rent (expense)
- Total payables (current liability)

## The accounting equation

$$\text{ASSETS} = \text{CAPITAL} + \text{LIABILITIES}$$

### Capital

Investment of funds with the intention of earning a return

### Drawings

Amounts withdrawn from the business by the owner

The accounting equation is based on the principle that an entity is separate from the owner, ie the business entity concept.

## Basic principles

Double entry bookkeeping is based on the same idea as the accounting equation.

- Every accounting transaction has two equal but opposite effects
- Equality of assets and liabilities plus capital is preserved

In a system of double entry bookkeeping every accounting event must be entered in ledger accounts both as a debit and as an equal but opposite credit.

### Debit

- An increase in an expense
- An increase in an asset
- A decrease in a liability

### Credit

- An increase in income
- An increase in a liability
- A decrease in an asset

## Double entry bookkeeping

The rules of double entry bookkeeping are best learnt by considering the cash book.

A credit entry indicates a payment made by the business; the matching debit entry is then made in an account denoting an expense paid, an asset purchased or a liability settled.

A debit entry in the cash book indicates cash received by the business; the matching credit entry is then made in an account denoting revenue received, a liability created or an asset realised.

# The Journal

- The journal is a book of prime entry
- It is used for transactions which are not recorded in any of the other books of prime entry

Format of journal entries is as follows:

| Date | | Debit | Credit |
|------|------|-------|--------|
| | | $ | $ |
| DEBIT | A/c to be debited | X | |
| CREDIT | A/c to be credited | | X |

Narrative to explain transaction

**Remember that the journal is used to keep a record of unusual movements between accounts.**

## Day book analysis

Entries in the day books are totalled and analysed before posting to the nominal ledger.

Note that day books are often analysed as in the following extract (date, customer name and reference not shown).

| Total invoiced | Calculator sales | Book sales |
|---|---|---|
| $ | $ | $ |
| 340 | 160 | 180 |
| 120 | 70 | 50 |
| 600 | 350 | 250 |
| 1,060 | 580 | 480 |

To identify sales by product, total sales would be entered ('posted') as follows:

|  |  | $ | $ |
|---|---|---|---|
| DEBIT | Receivables a/c | 1,060 |  |
| CREDIT | Sales: Calculators |  | 580 |
|  | Sales: Books |  | 480 |

Other books of prime entry are analysed in a similar way.

## Trade accounts receivable and payable

### Trade account receivable

A customer who buys goods without paying for them straight away (an asset)

Also known as a **debtor**.

### Trade account payable

A person to whom a business owes money (a liability)

Also known as a **creditor**.

## Receivables and payables ledgers

To keep track of individual customer and supplier balances it is common to maintain subsidiary ledgers called the **receivables ledger** and the **payables ledger**. Each account in these ledgers represents the balance owed by or to an **individual** customer or supplier.

These receivables and payables ledgers are usually kept purely for reference and are therefore known as **memorandum records**. They do not form part of the double entry system.

However, some computerised accounting packages treat the receivables and payables ledgers as part of the double entry system, in which case separate control accounts are not kept.

Entries to the receivables ledger are made as follows:

- When making an entry in the sales day book, an entry is then made on the debit side of the customer's account in the receivables ledger.
- When cash is received and an entry made in the cash book, an entry is also made on the credit side of the customer's account in the receivables ledger.

The payables ledger operates in much the same way.

# 6: From trial balance to financial statements

## Topic List

The trial balance

The statement of profit or loss

Statement of financial position

Preparing financial statements

*The balances need to be extracted from the ledger accounts and entered into the trial balance.*

*Double entry bookkeeping dictates that the trial balance will have the same amount on the debit side as there is on the credit side.*

## Balancing ledger accounts

At the end of an accounting period a balance is determined on each ledger account.

- Total all debits and credits
- Debits exceed credits = debit balance
- Credits exceed debits = credit balance

An example of balancing a ledger account is shown below.

RECEIVABLES

| | $ | | $ |
|---|---|---|---|
| Sales | 10,000 | Cash | 8,000 |
| | | Balance c/d | 2,000 |
| | 10,000 | | 10,000 |
| Balance b/d | 2,000 | | |

This account has a debit balance of $2,000.

## Trial balance

The balances are then collected in a trial balance. If the double entry is correct, total debits = total credits.

### Errors

A trial balance does not guarantee accuracy. It will not pick up the following errors.

- Compensating errors
- Errors of commission
- Errors of omission
- Errors of principle

An example of a trial is shown below.

```
ABC TRADERS
TRIAL BALANCE AS AT 30 JUNE 20X7
                              $          $
Sales                                   35,000
Purchases                  13,000
Receivables                 2,000
Payables                                 1,500
Cash                       10,000
Capital                                 10,000
Loan                                    10,000
Rent                        4,000
Sundry expenses             3,500
Loan interest               1,000
Drawings                    5,000
Fixtures and fittings      18,000
                           _____     _____
                           56,500     56,500
```

| The trial balance | The statement of profit or loss | Statement of financial position | Preparing financial statements |

## Statement of profit or loss

First open up a ledger account for the statement of profit or loss. Continuing our example for ABC Traders this ledger account is shown below, together with the rent account to illustrate how balances are transferred to it at the end of the year.

| STATEMENT OF PROFIT OR LOSS | | | | RENT | | | |
|---|---|---|---|---|---|---|---|
| | $ | | $ | | $ | | $ |
| Purchases | 13,000 | Sales | 35,000 | Cash | 4,000 | SPL | 4,000 |
| Rent | 4,000 | | | | 4,000 | | 4,000 |
| Sundry expenses | 3,500 | | | | | | |
| Loan interest | 1,000 | | | | | | |

This could be rearranged as follows to arrive at the financial statement with which you are familiar.

```
ABC TRADERS
STATEMENT OF PROFIT OR LOSS
FOR THE YEAR ENDED 30 JUNE 20X7
                                        $              $
Sales                                               35,000
Cost of sales (here = purchases)                    13,000
Gross profit                                        22,000
Expenses
    Rent                               4,000
    Sundry expenses                    3,500
    Loan interest                      1,000
                                                     8,500
Net profit                                          13,500
```

## Statement of financial position

The statement of financial position is prepared by following these steps.

- Balance off the accounts relating to assets and liabilities, following the receivables example shown above.

- Transfer the balances on the drawings account and the statement of profit or loss ($13,500) to the capital account as follows:

DRAWINGS

| | $ | | $ |
|---|---|---|---|
| Cash | 5,000 | Capital | 5,000 |

STATEMENT OF PROFIT OR LOSS

| | $ | | $ |
|---|---|---|---|
| Purchases | 13,000 | Sales | 35,000 |
| Rent | 4,000 | | |
| Sundry expenses | 3,500 | | |
| Loan interest | 1,000 | | |
| Capital a/c | 13,500 | | |
| | 35,000 | | 35,000 |

CAPITAL

| | $ | | $ |
|---|---|---|---|
| Drawings | 5,000 | Cash | 10,000 |
| Balance c/d | 18,500 | SPL | 13,500 |
| | 23,500 | | 23,500 |

The statement of financial position can then be prepared as follows.

```
ABC TRADERS
STATEMENT OF FINANCIAL POSITION AS AT 30 JUNE 20X7
                                    $           $
Non-current assets
  Fixtures and fittings                       18,000

Current assets
  Receivables                     2,000
  Cash                           10,000
                                              12,000
                                              30,000
                                              ======
Proprietor's capital                          18,500

Current liabilities
  Payables                        1,500
  Loan                           10,000
                                              11,500
                                              30,000
                                              ======
```

## Accounting process overview

This diagram summarises the topics you have revised so far. Look at it just before your exam – everything should fall into place.

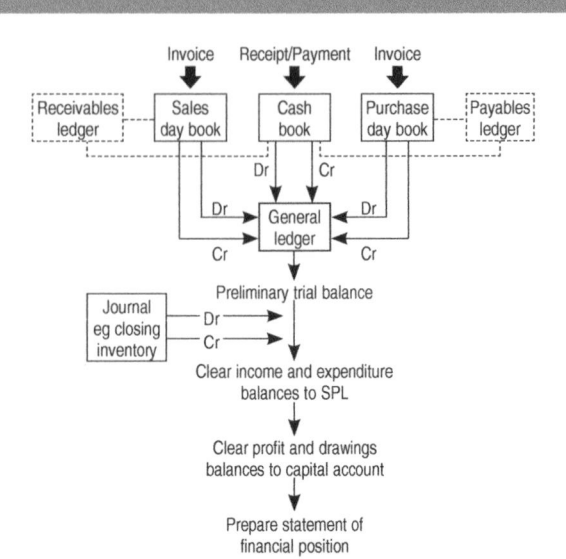

# 7: Inventory

## Topic List

*This is an important chapter, it covers a standard (IAS 2) and the complexities surrounding the inventory figure.*

*Remember, the inventory figure affects both the statement of financial position and the statement of profit or loss.*

## Formula for the cost of goods sold

|  | $ |
|---|---|
| Opening inventory value | X |
| Add: Purchases (or production costs) | X |
|  | X |
| Less: Closing inventory value | (X) |
| Cost of goods sold | X |

### Carriage inwards

- Cost paid by purchaser of having goods transported to his business
- Added to cost of purchases

### Carriage outwards

- Cost to the seller, paid by the seller, of having goods transported to customer
- Is a selling and distribution expense

## Entries during the year

During the year, purchases are recorded by the following entry:

DEBIT     Purchases     $ amount bought
CREDIT     Cash or payables     $ amount bought

The inventory account is **not touched at all**.

## Entries at year-end

The first thing to do is to transfer the purchases account balance to the statement of profit or loss:

DEBIT     SPL     $ total purchases
CREDIT     Purchases     $ total purchases

The balance on the inventory account is still the **opening inventory balance**. This must also be transferred to the statement of profit or loss:

DEBIT     SPL     $ opening inventory
CREDIT     Inventory     $ opening inventory

The exact reverse entry is made for the **closing inventory** (which will be next year's opening inventory):

DEBIT     Inventory     $ closing inventory
CREDIT     SPL     $ closing inventory

## Counting inventories

In order to make the entry for the closing inventory, businesses need to know what is held at the year-end. They find this out **not** from the accounting records, but by going into the warehouse and actually counting the boxes on the shelves.

Some businesses keep detailed records of inventory coming in and going out, so as not to have to count everything on the last day of the year. These records are **not** part of the double entry system.

## Cost

Can use per IAS 2:

- FIFO
- Average cost (both periodic weighted average and continuous weighted average)

LIFO is not permitted.

## Valuation

Inventories must be valued at the **lower** of:

- Cost
- Net realisable value (NRV)

## NRV

| | |
|---|---|
| Expected selling price | X |
| Less costs to get items | |
| ready for sale | (X) |
| selling costs | (X) |
| NRV | X |

## IAS 2

- Inventories should be measured at the lower of cost and net realisable value – the comparison between the two should ideally be made separately for each item
- Cost is the cost incurred in the normal course of business in bringing the product to its present location and condition, including production overheads and costs of conversion
- Inventory can include raw materials, work in progress, finished goods, goods purchased for resale
- FIFO and average cost are allowed
- LIFO is not allowed

**Note.** Inventory excludes construction contracts in progress (IAS 11), financial instruments (IASs 32 and 39), agricultural products (IAS 41) and mineral ores.

**Inventories** are assets:

- Held for sale in the ordinary course of business;
- In the process of production for such sale; or
- In the form of materials or supplies to be consumed in the production process or in the rendering of services.

**Net realisable value** (NRV) is the expected selling price in the ordinary course of business less the estimated costs of completion and the estimated costs necessary to make the sale.

# 8: Tangible non-current assets

## Topic List

Capital and revenue expenditure

IAS 16

Depreciation

Non-current asset disposals

Revaluations

Disclosure

The asset register

*Non-current assets are assets bought by a business for continuing use, and are expected to be held for more than one accounting period. Tangible non-current assets have physical form (eg buildings or equipment).*

*You must be able to account for revaluations and disposals and to discuss IAS 16's main requirements.*

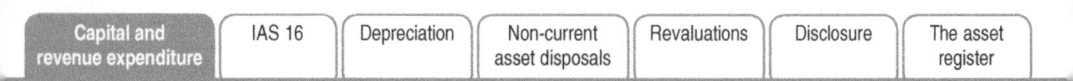

Distinction between capital
and revenue expenditure

Capital expenditure results in the acquisition of non-current assets, or an increase in their earning capacity.

Revenue expenditure is incurred for the purpose of trade or to maintain the existing earning capacity of the non-current assets.

## IAS 16

- **Initial measurement** – at cost
- **Components of cost**
  - Purchase price (including import duties, excluding trade discount, recoverable sales tax)
  - Initial estimate of dismantling and restoration costs
  - Directly attributable costs, eg:

    (i) Site preparation
    (ii) Installation and assembly costs
    (iii) Professional fees

    (iv) Delivery and handling costs
    (v) Costs of testing whether working properly
    (vi) Staff costs arising directly from the construction or acquisition of the asset

- **Subsequent expenditure**
  - Added to carrying amount if improves condition beyond previous performance
- **Repairs and maintenance** costs are **expensed**.

## Depreciation – accruals concept

Is a process of spreading the original cost of a non-current asset over the accounting periods in which its economic benefit will be consumed.

## Two methods

### Straight line

$$Dep'n = \frac{cost - residual\ value}{useful\ life}$$

### Reducing balance

$$Dep'n = carrying\ value \times reducing\ balance\%$$

The double entry for depreciation is as follows.

DEBIT   Depreciation expense (SPL)
CREDIT  Accumulated depreciation (SOFP)

## Change in expected life

If after a period of an asset's life it is realised that the original useful life has been changed, then the depreciation charge needs to be adjusted. The revised charge from that date becomes:

$$\frac{Carrying\ amount\ at\ revised\ date}{Remaining\ useful\ life}$$

## Disposal

On disposal of an asset a profit or loss will arise depending on whether disposal proceeds are greater or less than the carrying value of the asset.

- If proceeds > CV = profit
- If proceeds < CV = loss

### Double entry for a disposal

- Eliminate cost

  DEBIT      Disposals
  CREDIT      Non-current assets

- Eliminate accumulated depreciation

  DEBIT      Accumulated depreciation
  CREDIT      Disposals

- Account for sales proceeds

  DEBIT      Cash
  CREDIT      Disposals

  Or if the disposal is in a part exchange deal:

  DEBIT      Non-current assets
  CREDIT      Disposals

  with asset exchange value

- Transfer balance on disposals account to the statement of profit or loss

IAS 16 allows a choice between:

- Keeping assets at cost
- Revaluing to fair value

Fair value may give fairer view on value of the assets held in the business

## Revaluation

A revaluation is recorded as follows:

DEBIT    Non-current asset
(revalued amount less original cost)

DEBIT    Accumulated depreciation
(total depreciation to date)

CREDIT   Revaluation surplus
(revalued amount less carrying value)

Revalued assets are depreciated over their remaining useful economic life.

## Disclosure

With regard to disclosure, a proforma non-current asset note is shown here.

|  | Total $'000 | Land and buildings $'000 | Plant and equipment $'000 |
|---|---|---|---|
| *Cost or valuation* |  |  |  |
| At 1 January 20X7 | 160 | 100 | 60 |
| Revaluation surplus | 20 | 20 | – |
| Additions in year | 50 | 30 | 20 |
| Disposals in year | (45) | (15) | (30) |
| At 31 December 20X7 | 185 | 135 | 50 |
| *Depreciation* |  |  |  |
| At 1 January 20X7 | 30 | 20 | 10 |
| Charge for year | 7 | 5 | 2 |
| Eliminated on disposals | (3) | – | (3) |
| At 31 December 20X7 | 34 | 25 | 9 |
| *Carrying value* |  |  |  |
| At 31 December 20X7 | 151 | 110 | 41 |
| At 1 January 20X7 | 130 | 80 | 50 |

The asset register contains details of each non-current asset owned by the business.

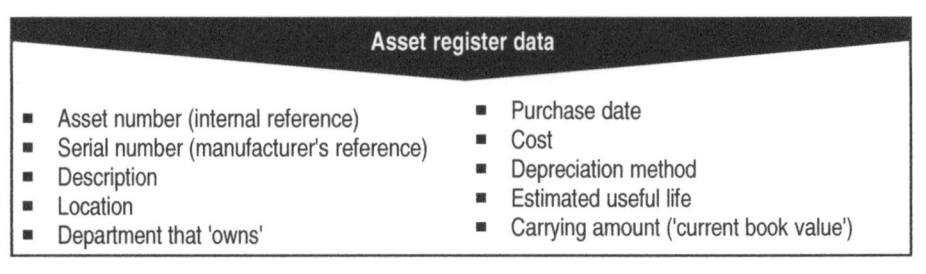

| Asset register data |
| --- |

- Asset number (internal reference)
- Serial number (manufacturer's reference)
- Description
- Location
- Department that 'owns'

- Purchase date
- Cost
- Depreciation method
- Estimated useful life
- Carrying amount ('current book value')

The asset register should be reconciled to the relevant nominal ledger accounts.

# 9: Intangible non-current assets

## Topic List

Intangible non-current assets

Research and development costs

*Intangible non-current assets are non-current assets with no physical substance.*

*The accounting treatment for intangible assets is governed by IAS 38.*

| Intangible non-current assets | Research and development costs |

## Intangible non-current assets

Non-current assets which have a value to the entity but no physical substance.

### Examples

- Goodwill
- Patents and trade names
- Deferred development costs

## Amortisation

Intangible assets must be amortised systematically over their useful life. An intangible asset with an **indefinite** useful life is **not** amortised but should be reviewed each year for impairment.

| Disclosure |
| --- |
| ■ Method of amortisation used |
| ■ Useful life of the assets or amortisation rate used |
| ■ Gross carrying value, accumulated amortisation and accumulated impairment losses at beginning and end of period |
| ■ Movements during the period |
| ■ Carrying amount of internally-generated intangible assets |

## IAS 38 Intangible assets

- Pure or basic research
- Applied research
- Development expenditure must be capitalised if all criteria stated under IAS 38 can be demonstrated
- Financial statements should show a reconciliation of the carrying amount of intangible assets at the beginning and end of the period

→ All costs written off as incurred

P – **Probable** future economic benefits

I – **Intention** to complete the intangible asset and use or sell it

R – the availability of **Resources** to complete the development and use or sell

A – **Ability** to use or sell

T – **Technical** feasibility of completing the asset

E – reliable measurement of **Expenditure**

# 10: Accruals and prepayments

## Topic List

Accruals and prepayments

*This chapter covers the adjustments which need to be made to expenses in order to reflect the true level of profits for the accounting period.*

## Accrual

Expenses charged against the profits of a period even though they have not yet been paid for

## Prepayment

Payments made in one period but charged to the later period to which they relate

## Prepayment

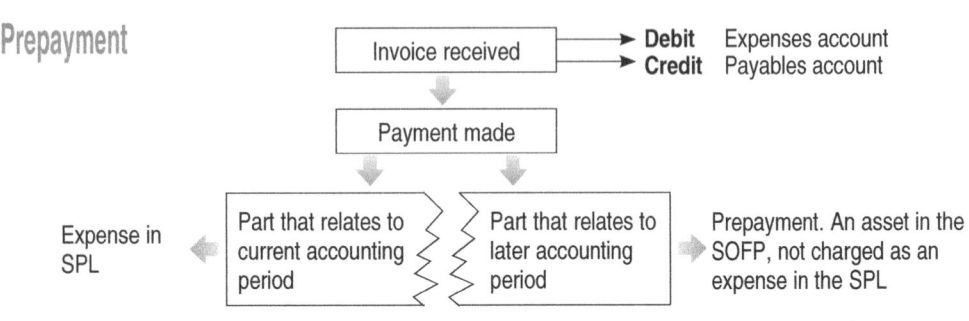

The amounted debited to the SOFP will hit the SPL in the next period.

## Accruals

> Expense incurred – No invoice yet

Part relating to current accounting period is an accrual

| | |
|---|---|
| **Debit** | SPL expense |
| **Credit** | SOFP payables (liability) |

**Remember that the financial statements are prepared on an accruals basis.**

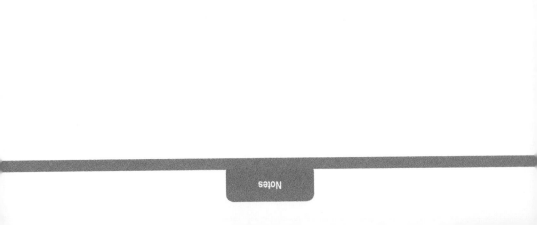

Notes

# 11: Provisions and contingencies

*This standard is a key area of the syllabus. Learn how to apply it. The most important thing you should do is learn the definitions and recognition criteria, and apply these to various cases.*

## Provision

A liability of uncertain timing or amount

### Recognition criteria

A provision should be recognised when:

- The entity has a present obligation as a result of a past event; and
- It is probable a transfer of economic benefits will be required to settle the obligation and
- A reliable estimate can be made of the obligation

The amount recognised for the provision should be the best estimate.

## Contingent Liability

(1) A possible obligation that arises from past events, whose existence will be confirmed by the occurrence or non-occurrence of future events not wholly in the entity's control.

(2) A present obligation not recognised because:

- It is not probable that settlement of the obligation will be required
- The amount cannot be measured

## Contingent Asset

A possible asset that arises from past events and whose existence will be confirmed by the occurrence of one or more uncertain future events not wholly within the entity's control.

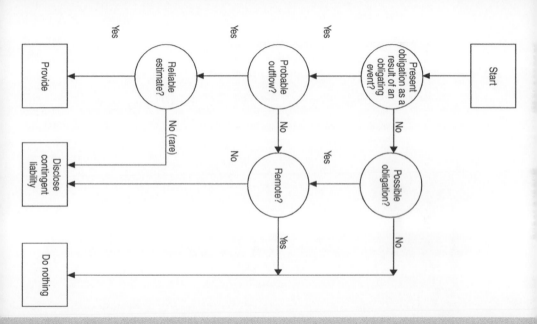

**Accounting treatment for provisions and contingencies**

| Provisions | Contingent liability | Contingent asset |
|---|---|---|

A provision should be recognised as a liability in the financial statements:

DEBIT   Expenses (SPL)
CREDIT   Provisions (SFP)

A contingent liability must not be recognised as a liability in the financial statements.

Instead it should be disclosed in the notes to the accounts, unless the possibility of an outflow of economic benefits is remote.

A contingent asset must not be recognised as an asset in the financial statements.

Instead it should be disclosed in the notes to the accounts if it is probable that the economic benefits associated with the asset will flow to the entity.

# 12: Irrecoverable debts and allowances

## Topic List

Irrecoverable debts and receivables allowances

Accounting for irrecoverable debts and receivables allowances

*This chapter looks at adjustments required where the entity expects that credit customers will not pay the amounts they owe to the entity.*

# Irrecoverable debts and receivables allowances

A receivable should only be classed as an asset if it is recoverable.

## Irrecoverable debts

If definitely irrecoverable, it should be written off to the statement of profit or loss as an irrecoverable debt.

DEBIT    Irrecoverable debt expense (SPL)

CREDIT   Trade receivables (SOFP)

## Receivables allowances

If uncertainty exists as to the recoverability of the debt, an allowance should be set up. This is offset against the receivables balance on the statement of financial position.

DEBIT    Irrecoverable debt expense (SPL)

CREDIT   Allowance for receivables (SOFP)

## Allowance for receivables

When calculating the allowance to be made, the following order applies.

|  | $ |
|---|---|
| Receivables balance per receivables control account | X |
| Less irrecoverable debts written off | (X) |
| Balance on which allowance is calculated | X |

If a reduction in the receivables allowance is required, then:

DEBIT    Allowance for receivables (SOFP)
CREDIT   Irrecoverable debts expense (SPL)

**Note.** Only the **movement** in the allowance needs to be charged or credited to the SPL.

|  | $ |
|---|---|
| Allowance required | X |
| Existing allowance | (X) |
| Increase/(decrease) required | X/(X) |

## Subsequent recovery of debts

If an irrecoverable debt is recovered, having previously been written off, then:

DEBIT    Cash (SOFP)
CREDIT   Irrecoverable debts expense (SPL)

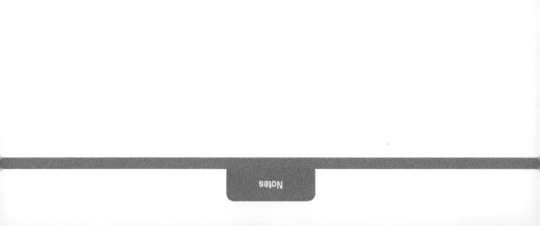

Notes

# 13: Sales tax

## Topic List

Nature and collection of sales tax

Accounting for sales tax

*In this chapter we first look at what sales tax is, and then we consider the accounting treatment for it.*

*In your exam, a sales tax could easily be examined as part of another topic.*

## Sales tax

Is an indirect tax levied on the sale of goods and services

Administered by tax authorities

Can have a number of rates, eg standard rate, reduced rate

## Output sales tax

Sales tax charged by the business on goods/services

Greater than input?
Pay difference to tax authorities

Greater than output?
Refund due to business

## Input sales tax

Sales tax on purchases made by the business

## a — Credit sales

(i) Include sales tax in sales day book; analyse it separately.

(ii) Include gross receipts from receivables in cash book; no need to show sales tax separately.

(iii) Exclude sales tax element from statement of profit or loss.

(iv) Credit sales tax control account with output sales tax element of sales invoices.

## b — Credit purchases

(i) Include sales tax in purchases day book; analyse it separately.

(ii) Include gross payments in cash book; no need to show sales tax separately.

(iii) Exclude recoverable sales tax from statement of profit or loss.

(iv) Include irrecoverable sales tax in statement of profit or loss.

(v) Debit sales tax control account with recoverable input sales tax element of credit purchases.

### c  Cash sales

(i) Include gross receipts in cash book; show sales tax separately.

(ii) Exclude sales tax element from statement of profit or loss.

(iii) Credit sales tax control account with output sales tax element of cash sales.

### d  Cash purchases

(i) Include gross payments in cash book: show sales tax separately.

(ii) Exclude recoverable sales tax from statement of profit or loss.

(iii) Include irrecoverable sales tax in statement of profit or loss.

(iv) Debit sales tax control account with recoverable input sales tax element of cash purchases.

# 14: Control accounts

## Topic List

What are control accounts?

Discounts

The operation of control accounts

The purpose of control accounts

*A control account is an account in the nominal ledger in which a record is kept of the total value of a number of similar but individual items.*

*Control accounts are used mainly for trade receivables and payables, but they could also be used for other areas.*

## What are control accounts

A control account is a **total** account.

- Its balance represents an asset or a liability which is the grand total of many individual assets or liabilities.

- These individual assets/liabilities must be separately detailed in subsidiary accounting records, but their total is conveniently available in the control account ready for immediate use.

Most businesses operate control accounts for trade receivables and payables, but such accounts may be useful in other areas too, eg sales tax.

With regard to the double entry relating to receivables and payables, note the following:

- The accounts of individuals are maintained **for information purposes only**.

- Entering a sales invoice, say, in the account of an individual receivable is **not part of the double entry** process.

## Two types

**Trade discount** – reduction in cost of goods eg regular customers, bulk discounts

**Cash/settlement discount** – reduction in amount payable, eg for cash or prompt payment

## Accounting treatment

**Received**: deduct from purchases

**Allowed**: deduct from sales invoice total, so that invoice is for price **less** discount

**Received**: included as other income

**Allowed**: if customer expected to take discount → measure at price **less** discount. If customer then does not take discount, recognise this amount in sales.

If customer **not** expected to take discount → measure at full amount

The invoices in the sales day book are totalled periodically and the total amount is posted as follows:

DEBIT   Receivables control account

CREDIT  Sales account

Similarly, the total of cash receipts from receivables is posted from the cash book to the credit side of the receivables control account.

In the same way, the payables control account is credited with the total purchase invoices logged in the purchase day book and debited with the total of cash payments to suppliers.

## Reasons for maintaining control accounts

- Check on the accuracy of the personal accounts in the receivables ledger.

- The control accounts provide a convenient total which can be used immediately in extracting a trial balance or preparing accounts.

- A reconciliation between the control account total and the receivables ledger will help to detect errors, thus providing an important control.

Receivables control account

| | | | |
|---|---|---|---|
| Balance b/d | X | Cash rec'd | X |
| Sales | X | Returns inwards | X |
| Dishonoured cheques | X | Irrecoverable debts | X |
| Interest charged on late accounts | X | Contra with payables | X |
| | | Balance c/d | X |
| | $\overline{X}$ | | $\overline{X}$ |
| Balance b/d | X | | |

### Payables control account

| | | | |
|---|---|---|---|
| Cash paid | X | Balance b/d | X |
| Discounts received | X | Purchases | X |
| Contra with rec'ables | X | Interest on overdue | |
| Returns outwards | X | accounts | X |
| Balance c/d | $\underline{X}$ | | |
| | $\underline{\overline{X}}$ | | $\underline{X}$ |
| | | | $\overline{X}$ |
| | | Balance b/d | X |

### Reconciling control a/cs with memorandum ledgers

**Step 1** – Correct the total of the balances from the memorandum ledger

**Step 2** – Correct the control a/c balance

**Note.** The corrected control a/c balance appears in the final accounts.

Possible reasons for credit balances on receivables ledger accounts, or for debit balances on payables ledger accounts:

- Overpayment of amount owed
- Return of goods
- Payment in advance
- Posting errors

# 15: Bank reconciliations

## Topic List

Bank statement and cash book

Bank reconciliation

*It is very likely that you will get a question on bank reconciliations in your exam. With a small amount of practice you should be able to tackle any bank reconciliation thrown at you.*

## Bank reconciliation

A comparison of a bank statement with the cash book.

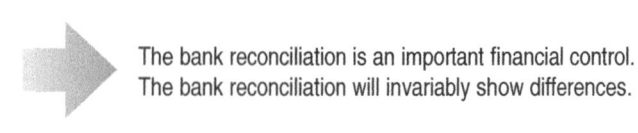

The bank reconciliation is an important financial control.
The bank reconciliation will invariably show differences.

### Differences on bank reconciliation

- Errors: More likely in the cash book.

- Omissions: Items on the bank statement not in the cash book (eg bank charges).

- Timing differences: Eg cheques issued and entered in the cash book but not yet presented at the bank.

## Proforming a bank reconciliation

**1** Correct the cash book

**2** Reconcile to the bank statement

### Corrected cash book

### Proforma bank reconciliation

#### CASH ACCOUNT

| | | | | |
|---|---|---|---|---|
| Balance b/f | X | Dishonoured cheque | X | |
| Bank interest | X | Bank charges | X | |
| | | Standing orders | X | |
| | | Direct debits | X | |
| | | Balance c/f | X | |
| | $\overline{X}$ | | $\overline{X}$ | |
| Corrected balance b/f | X | | | |

| | $ |
|---|---|
| Balance per bank statement | X |
| Less outstanding cheques | (X) |
| Plus outstanding lodgements | X |
| Plus/less bank errors | X/(X) |
| Balance per corrected cash book | X |

Corrected cash book balance is the cash balance that is shown in the SOFP.

Notes

# 16: Correction of errors

## Topic List

Types of error in accounting

The correction of errors

*There are often errors in trial balance figures, and these errors need to be corrected before the final accounts can be prepared.*

*It helps to know what kind of errors can be made in order that you can find them and correct them.*

## Types of error

### The main types of error are as follows

- Errors of transposition, eg writing $381 as $318 (the difference is divisible by 9)
- Errors of omission, eg receive supplier's invoice for $500 and do not record it in the books at all
- Errors of principle, eg treating capital expenditure as revenue expenditure
- Errors of commission, eg putting telephone expenses of $250 in the electricity expense account
- Compensating errors, eg both sales day book and purchases day book coincidentally undercast by $500

## Correction of errors

Errors can be corrected using the journal, but only those errors which required both a debit and an (equal) credit adjustment. Consider the following examples:

### Example

Accountant omits to record invoice from supplier for $2,000. This would be corrected by the following journal entry:

DEBIT    Purchases    $2,000
CREDIT  Payables           $2,000

A transaction previously omitted.

### Example

Accountant posts car insurance of $800 to motor vehicles account. Correct as follows:

DEBIT    Motor expenses    $800
CREDIT  Motor vehicles         $800

Correction of error of principle.

**A suspense account is a temporary account that is used in the following circumstances:**

1. The bookkeeper knows in which account to make the debit entry for a transaction but does not know where to make the corresponding credit entry (or vice versa)

   The credit is temporarily posted to the suspense account until the correct credit entry is known

2. A difference occurs in the trial balance caused by the incomplete recording of the double entry in respect of one or more transactions

   The difference is recorded in the suspense account and included in the trial balance, so restoring equality

Any balance on a suspense account must be eliminated. It is **never** included in the final financial statements.

## Example

Harry Perkins, sole trader, prepared his trial balance for the year ended 30 June 20X5. In order to balance the trial balance, he credited $7,452 to a suspense account.

He has since discovered the following errors:

1. Irrecoverable debts of $486 were posted to the irrecoverable debts account as $684

2. Credit sales totalling $7,500 had not been posted to the sales account

3. The balance on the accruals account of $404 had been omitted when the trial balance was prepared

4. In respect of telephone expenses of $650, the only entry to have been made was in the cash account

The balance would be cleared by writing up the suspense account as follows:

SUSPENSE ACCOUNT

| | $ | | $ |
|---|---|---|---|
| Irrecoverable debts (i) expense | 198 | B/d | 7,452 |
| Sales (ii) | 7,500 | Telephone (iv) | 650 |
| Accruals (iii) | 404 | | |
| | 8,102 | | 8,102 |

(i) The correct entry:

| | | $ | $ |
|---|---|---|---|
| DEBIT | Irrecoverable debts | 486 | |
| CREDIT | Receivables | | 486 |

The actual entry:

| | | $ | $ |
|---|---|---|---|
| DEBIT | Irrecoverable debts | 684 | |
| CREDIT | Receivables | | 486 |
| ∴ CREDIT | Suspense (balance) | | 198 |

To correct:

| | | $ | $ |
|---|---|---|---|
| DEBIT | Suspense | 198 | |
| CREDIT | Irrecoverable debts | | 198 |

(ii) The correct entry:

| | | $ | $ |
|---|---|---|---|
| DEBIT | Receivables | 7,500 | |
| CREDIT | Sales | | 7,500 |

The actual entry:

| | | $ | $ |
|---|---|---|---|
| DEBIT | Receivables | 7,500 | |
| ∴ CREDIT | Suspense | | 7,500 |

To correct:

| | | $ | $ |
|---|---|---|---|
| DEBIT | Suspense | 7,500 | |
| CREDIT | Sales | | 7,500 |

(iii) To correct:

| | | $ | $ |
|---|---|---|---|
| DEBIT | Suspense | 404 | |
| CREDIT | Accruals | | 404 |

(iv) To correct:

| | | $ | $ |
|---|---|---|---|
| DEBIT | Telephone | 650 | |
| CREDIT | Suspense | | 650 |

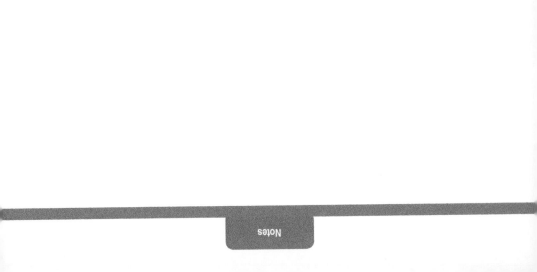
Notes

# 17: Incomplete records

## Topic List

Incomplete records questions

Accounting and business equations

Credit sales, purchases and cost of sales

Stolen or destroyed goods

Cash book

Accruals, prepayments and drawings

*This area is a very good test of your accounts preparation knowledge.*

*You need to know how the accounts fit together in order to fill the blanks.*

## Types of question

An incomplete records question may require competence in dealing with one or more of the following:

- Preparation of accounts from information in the question
- Theft of cash (balance on the cash in hand account is unknown)
- Theft or destruction of inventory (closing inventory is the unknown)
- Estimated figures, eg 'drawings are between $15 and $20 per week'
- Calculation of capital by means of net assets
- Calculation of profit by P = increase in net assets plus drawings minus increase in capital
- Calculation of year end inventory when the inventory count was done after the year end

## Accounting equation

- An examination question may provide information about the assets and liabilities of an entity at the beginning of a period, leaving you to calculate capital as the balancing figure.

- Remember:

  Assets = Capital + Liabilities So, rearranging this:

  Assets – liabilities = Proprietor's capital

## Business equation

- If you know opening and closing net assets, you can calculate profit for the year by using the business equation:

  Profit/(loss) = movement in net assets + drawings – capital introduced

## Credit sales and receivables

- The key lies in the formula linking sales, cash receipts and receivables.
- Remember:

  Opening receivables + sales − cash receipts = closing receivables

- Alternatively put all the workings into a control account to calculate the figure you want.

## Purchases and trade accounts payables

- Similarly you need a formula for linking purchases, cash payments and payables.

  Opening payables + purchases − cash payments = closing payables

- Use a control account.

### RECEIVABLES CONTROL ACCOUNT

| | $ | | $ |
|---|---|---|---|
| Opening receivables | X | Cash receipts | X |
| Sales | X | Closing receivables | X |
| | X | | X |

### PAYABLES CONTROL ACCOUNT

| | $ | | $ |
|---|---|---|---|
| Cash payments | X | Opening payables | X |
| Closing payables | X | Purchases | X |
| | X | | X |

## Gross margins and mark-ups

Other incomplete records problems revolve around the relationship between sales, cost of sales and gross profit. Bear in mind the crucial formula:

|  |  | $ |
|---|---|---|
| | Sales | 100 |
| **Less** | Cost of sales | 25 |
| **Equals** | Gross profit | 75 |

**Mark-up** is profit as a % of **cost**

eg $33\frac{1}{3}$% mark-up

|  |  | $ |
|---|---|---|
| Sales | $133\frac{1}{3}$% | 80 |
| COS | 100% | (60) |
| Gross profit | $33\frac{1}{3}$% | 20 |

**Margin** is profit as a % of **sales**

eg 25% margin

|  |  | $ |
|---|---|---|
| Sales | 100% | 80 |
| COS | 75% | (60) |
| Gross profit | 25% | 20 |

## Stolen goods or goods destroyed

The cost of goods stolen/destroyed can be calculated as follows:

|  | $ |
|---|---|
| Cost of goods sold based on gross profit margin or mark-up | A |
| Cost of goods sold calculated using standard formula (ie opening inventory plus purchases less closing inventory) | (B) |
| Difference (lost/stolen inventory) | C |

- If no goods have been lost, A and B should be the same and therefore C should be nil.

- If goods have been lost, B will be larger than A, because some goods which have been purchased were neither sold nor remaining in inventory, ie they have been lost.

- Stolen or lost inventory is accounted for in two ways depending on whether the goods were insured.

| If insured: | If not insured: |
|---|---|
| DEBIT  Insurance claim account (receivable) | DEBIT  Expenses (eg Admin) |
| CREDIT Cost of sales | CREDIT Cost of sales |

# Cash book

Incomplete records problems often concern small retail entities where sales are mainly for cash. A two-column cash book is often the key to preparing final accounts.

- The bank column records cheques drawn on the business bank account and cheques received from customers and other sources

- The cash column records till receipts and any expenses or drawings paid out of till receipts before banking

| Debits (receipts) | | Credits (payments) | |
|---|---|---|---|
| Cash | Bank | Cash | Bank |
| $ | $ | $ | $ |

Don't forget that movements between cash and bank need to be recorded by contra entries. This will usually be cash receipts lodged in the bank (debit bank column, credit cash column), but could also be withdrawals of cash from the bank to top up the till (debit cash column, credit bank column).

Again, incomplete records problems will often feature an unknown figure to be derived. Enter in the credit of the cash column all amounts known to have been paid from till receipts: expenses, withdrawals, lodgements into bank. Enter in the debit of the cash column all receipts from cash customers or other cash sources.

- The balancing figure may then be a large debit, representing the value of cash sales if that is the unknown figure.

- Alternatively it may be a credit entry that is needed to balance, representing the amount of cash withdrawals or of cash stolen.

17: Incomplete records

## Accruals and prepayments

When there is an accrued expense or prepayment, the SPL charge can be calculated from the opening balance, the cash movement and the closing balance.

Sometimes it helps to use a 'T' account, eg as follows (for a rent payment).

RENT

|  | $ |  | $ |
|---|---|---|---|
| Prepayment: bal b/f | 700 | SPL (bal fig) | 9,000 |
| Cash | 9,300 | Prepayment: bal c/f | 1,000 |
|  | 10,000 |  | 10,000 |

## Drawings

Note three tricky points about drawings.

- Owner pays personal income into business bank account

    DEBIT    Cash
    CREDIT   Drawings

- Owner pays personal expenses out of business bank account or takes goods for personal use

    DEBIT    Drawings
    CREDIT   Cash/Purchases

- Wording of an exam question

    - 'Drawings approximately $40 per week'
      $\therefore$ Drawings for year = $40 \times 52 = $2,080

    - 'Drawings between $35 and $45 per week'
      $\therefore$ Drawings are a missing number to be calculated

# 18: Preparation of financial statements for sole traders

## Topic List

Preparation of final accounts

*A sole trader's accounts are prepared from the trial balance, including adjustments for things like accruals and irrecoverable debts where necessary, as well as clearing a suspense account.*

## Final accounts

You have now revised all areas necessary to prepare the final accounts of a sole trader. Areas you should be totally familiar with are as follows:

- Ledger accounts
- Trial balance
- Format of statement of profit or loss and statement of financial position

In addition, you should be able to deal with the following adjustments:

- Depreciation
- Inventory
- Accruals and prepayments
- Irrecoverable debts
- Allowance for receivables
- Profit/loss disposal of non-current assets

# 19: Introduction to company accounting

*This section looks at the basics of limited liability companies and how they differ from sole traders.*

## Topic List

Limited liability companies

Shares

Reserves

Bonus and rights issues

## Features

Limited liability companies offer limited liability to their owners (shareholders). If the company becomes insolvent, the maximum amount that an owner stands to lose is his share of the capital of the business. This is an attractive prospect to investors. Limited liability companies may be private or public. IAS 1 sets out a suggested format for financial statements.

- Owners = shareholders or members
- Large number of owners
- Owner/manager split
- Owners appoint directors to run business on their behalf
- Owners receive share of profits in form of dividends

### Disadvantages

- Compliance with national legislation
- Compliance with national accounting standards and/or IFRS
- Any formation or annual registration costs

### Funding

Companies are funded in the following ways:

- Retained profits
- Share capital
- Short term liabilities (trade accounts payable etc)
- Loan notes

## Shares

The proprietors' capital in a limited liability company consists of share capital. When a company is set up for the first time it issues shares, which are paid for by investors, who then become shareholders of the company.

Shares are denominated in units of 25 cents, 50 cents, $1 or whatever seems appropriate. This is referred to as their nominal value.

| Preferred shares are characterised as follows: |
| --- |
| ■ Rights depend on articles |
| ■ Right to fixed dividend with priority over ordinary shares |
| ■ Do not usually carry voting rights |
| ■ Generally priority for capital in winding up |
| ■ May be redeemable (loan) or irredeemable (equity) |

| Ordinary shares have the following characteristics: |
| --- |
| ■ No right to fixed dividend |
| ■ Entitled to remaining profits after preferred dividend |
| ■ Entitled to surplus on repayment of capital |

## Share capital

- **Authorised**. The maximum amount of share capital that a company is empowered to issue.
- **Issued.** The amount of share capital that has been issued to shareholders. The amount of issued capital cannot exceed the amount of authorised capital.
- **Called up.** When shares are issued or allotted, a company does not always expect to be paid the full amount of the issue price at once. it might instead call up only a part of the issue price, and call up the remainder later.
- **Paid-up.** Called up capital that has been paid.
- **Market value.** This is the price at which someone is prepared to purchase the share from an existing shareholder. It is different from nominal value.

The following are the main types of share issue:

- New issue at par or at a premium
- Bonus/scrip/capitalisation issue
- Rights issue

## Loan notes

Companies may issue loan notes. These are long term liabilities not capital. They differ from shares as follows:

- Shareholder = owner; noteholder = payable
- Loan note interest **must** be paid; dividends need not be
- Loan notes often secured on company assets

## Reserves

Revenue reserves consist of distributable profits and can be paid out as dividends.

- Retained earnings
- Others, as the directors decide, eg general reserve

Capital reserves are not available for distribution. They include the following:

- **Share premium.** Whenever shares are issued for a consideration in excess of their nominal value, such a premium shall be credited to a share premium account.
- Share premium account can be used to:
    - Issue bonus shares
    - Write off formation expenses and premium on the redemption of shares and loan notes
    - Write off the expenses on a new issue of shares/loan notes and the discount on the issue of loan notes
- **Revaluation surplus.** Created when a company revalues one or more of its non-current assets.
- **Statutory reserves.** The law requires the company to set up these.

Limited liability companies | Shares | Reserves | **Bonus and rights issues**

## Bonus issue

A bonus (or capitalisation) issue uses reserves to pay for the issue of share capital.

### Example

Issue of 5,000 new $1 shares

| | |
|---|---|
| Debit Reserves (share premium or retained earnings) | $5,000 |
| Credit Share capital | $5,000 |

## Rights issue

A rights issue enables existing shareholders to acquire further shares.

### Example

Issue of 5,000 new $1 shares at $1.50 per share

| | |
|---|---|
| Debit Cash | $7,500 |
| Credit Share capital | $5,000 |
| Credit Share premium | $2,500 |

# 20: Preparation of financial statements for companies

## Topic List

IAS 1

IFRS 15

*This section looks at limited liability company financial statements.*

*Limited liability company financial statements are more comprehensive as there are more stakeholders who wish to know how the business is performing.*

ABC CO
STATEMENT OF FINANCIAL POSITION
AS AT 31 DECEMBER 20X2

| | 20X2 $ | 20X2 $ | 20X1 $ | 20X1 $ |
|---|---|---|---|---|
| Assets | | | | |
| Non-current assets | | | | |
| Property, plant and equipment | X | | X | |
| Goodwill | X | | X | |
| Other intangible assets | X | | X | |
| | | X | | X |
| Current assets | | | | |
| Inventories | X | | X | |
| Trade receivables | X | | X | |
| Other current assets | X | | X | |
| Cash and cash equivalents | X | | X | |
| | X | | X | |
| | | X | | X |
| Total assets | | X | | X |
| Equity and liabilities | | | | |
| Equity | | | | |
| Share capital | X | | X | |
| Retained earnings/(losses) | X | | X | |
| Other components of equity | X | | X | |
| | | X | | X |
| Total equity | | X | | X |
| Non-current liabilities | | | | |
| Long-term borrowings | X | | X | |
| Long-term provisions | X | | X | |
| | | X | | X |
| Current liabilities | | | | |
| Trade and other payables | X | | X | |
| Short-term borrowings | X | | X | |
| Current portion of long-term borrowings | X | | X | |
| Current tax payable | X | | X | |
| | X | | X | |
| | | X | | X |
| Total equity and liabilities | | X | | X |

# ABC CO
## STATEMENT OF PROFIT OR LOSS AND OTHER COMPREHENSIVE INCOME
### FOR THE YEAR ENDED 31 DECEMBER 20X2

|  | 20X2 | 20X1 |
|---|---|---|
|  | $ | $ |
| Revenue | X | X |
| Cost of sales | (X) | (X) |
| Gross profit | X | X |
| Other income | X | X |
| Distribution costs | (X) | (X) |
| Administrative expenses | (X) | (X) |
| Other expenses | (X) | (X) |
| Finance cost | (X) | (X) |
| *Profit before tax* | X | X |
| Income tax expense | (X) | (X) |
| *Profit for the year* | X | X |
| | | |
| *Other comprehensive income:* | | |
| Gains on property revaluation | X | X |
| | | |
| *Total comprehensive income for the year* | X | X |

ABC CO
STATEMENT OF CHANGES IN EQUITY FOR THE YEAR ENDED 31 DECEMBER 20X2

| | Share capital $ | Retained earnings $ | Revaluation surplus $ | Total $ |
|---|---|---|---|---|
| Balance at 1 January 20X2 | X | X | X | X |
| | | | | |
| Changes in equity for 20X2 | | | | |
| Issue of share capital | X | | | X |
| Dividends | | (X) | | (X) |
| Total comprehensive income for the year | | X | X | X |
| Balance at 31 December 20X2 | X | X | X | X |

## IFRS 15 *Revenue from Contracts with Customers*

### Recognition

Revenue is recognised when the entity has **transferred control** of goods and services to the buyer.

Control is 'the ability to **direct the use** of, and **obtain** substantially all of the remaining **benefits** from, the asset.'

IFRS 15 covers revenue from:

- Sale of goods
- Rendering of services

### Measurement

The amount of revenue is usually decided by the agreement of buyer and seller. However, the revenue is **measured** as the transaction price. If a cash/settlement discount is likely to be taken, then initial measurement is for the price less the discount.

Notes

# 21: Events after the reporting period

## Topic List

IAS 10

*This standard is a key area of the syllabus. You need to be able to identify whether or not any adjustments will be required in the financial statements as a result of events occurring after the reporting period.*

**Events after the reporting period**

Occur between the reporting date and the date on which the financial statements are authorised for issue.

**Adjusting events**

Provide additional evidence of conditions existing at the reporting date.

**Standard accounting**

Change the figures in the financial statements if the event is material and either it is an adjusting event or the going concern concept is no longer appropriate.

**Non-adjusting events**

Concern conditions which did not exist at the reporting date.

**Standard accounting**

Disclose an event in a note if it is material and is a non-adjusting event.

**Events after authorisation of the accounts**

The directors should consider publishing these if material.

## Examples

| Adjusting events | Non adjusting events |
|---|---|
| ■ Non-current assets. Determination of purchase price or proceeds of sale.<br><br>■ Inventories. Evidence of NRV.<br><br>■ Receivables. Renegotiation by or insolvency of trade accounts receivable.<br><br>■ Settlement of insurance claims.<br><br>■ Discoveries of error or fraud. | ■ Issues of shares.<br><br>■ Purchases/sales of non-current assets and investments.<br><br>■ Loss or drop in value of non-current assets or inventories occurring after the year end.<br><br>■ Expansion or contraction of trade.<br><br>■ Government action or strikes.<br><br>■ Dividends declared after the reporting date. |

Notes

## Topic List

IAS 7 Statement of cash flows

*Profit is not the same as cash. The statement of cash flows allows us to assess the quality of profit. How quickly does the profit figure get translated into a healthy cash balance?*

*It is possible for a profitable firm to collapse due to poor cash flows.*

## Purpose

A statement of cash flows shows the effect of an entity's commercial transactions on its cash balance.

It is thought that users of accounts can readily understand cash flows, as opposed to statements of profit or loss and statements of financial position, which are subject to manipulation by the use of different accounting policies.

## Format

IAS 7 Statement of cash flows splits cash flows into the following headings:

- Cash flows from operating activities
- Cash flows from investing activities
- Cash flows from financing activities

The IAS requires a reconciliation of cash and cash equivalents.

## STATEMENT OF CASH FLOWS
## YEAR ENDED 20X7 (INDIRECT METHOD)

|  | $m | $m |
|---|---|---|
| *Cash flows from operating activities* |  |  |
| Net profit before taxation |  | 3,390 |
| Adjustments for: |  |  |
| Depreciation | 450 |  |
| Investment income | (500) |  |
| Interest expense | 400 |  |
| Operating profit before working capital changes |  | 3,740 |
| Increase in trade and other receivables | (500) |  |
| Decrease in inventories | 1,050 |  |
| Decrease in trade payables | (1,740) |  |
| Cash generated from operations |  | 2,550 |
| Interest paid | (270) |  |
| Income taxes paid | (720) |  |
| Net cash from operating activities |  | 1,560 |
|  |  |  |
| *Cash flows from investing activities* |  |  |
| Purchase of property, plant and equipment | (900) |  |
| Proceeds from sale of equipment | 20 |  |
| Interest received | 200 |  |
| Dividends received | 200 |  |
| Net cash used in investing activities |  | (480) |
|  |  |  |
| *Cash flows from financing activities* |  |  |
| Proceeds from issuance of share capital | 250 |  |
| Proceeds from long-term borrowings | 250 |  |
| Dividends paid * | (1,290) |  |
| Net cash used in financing activities |  | (790) |
| Net increase in cash and cash equivalents |  | 290 |
| Cash and cash equivalents at beginning of period (Note) |  | 120 |
| Cash and cash equivalents at end of period (Note) |  | 410 |

\* This could also be shown as an operating cash flow

**Note. Cash and cash equivalents** consist of cash on hand and balances with banks, and investments in money marketing instruments. Cash and cash equivalents included in the cash flow statement comprise the following balance sheet amounts.

|  | 20X7 | 20X8 |
|---|---|---|
|  | $m | $m |
| Cash on hand and balances with banks | 40 | 25 |
| Short-term investments | 370 | 95 |
| Cash and cash equivalents | 410 | 120 |

The company has undrawn borrowing facilities of $2,000, of which only $700 may be used for future expansion.

This proforma is for the **indirect method**.
The **direct method** proforma is the same except for the first part which appears as follows.

|  | $ | $ |
|---|---|---|
| Cash receipts from customers |  | X |
| Cash paid to suppliers and employees |  | (X) |
| Cash generated from operations |  | X |
| Interest paid |  | (X) |
| Income taxes paid |  | (X) |
| Net cash from operating activities |  | X |

**Examination questions will probably require the indirect method. If the direct method is required, the necessary information will be given to you.**

| Advantages | Disadvantages |
|---|---|
| ☑ Business survival needs cash | ☒ The disadvantages of cash flow accounting are basically the opposite of advantages of accruals accounting, |
| ☑ Cash flow is more objective than profit | |
| ☑ Trade accounts payable need to know if they will be paid | ☒ For example, cash flow does *not* match income and expenditure in the statement of profit or loss. |
| ☑ More comparability between entities | |
| ☑ Better basis for decision making | |
| ☑ Easy to understand, prepare and audit | |

## Criticisms of IAS 7

- Inclusion of cash equivalents does not reflect the way businesses are managed.
- The requirement that a cash equivalent has to be within three months of maturity is unrealistic.
- Management of cash equivalents is not distinguished from other investment decisions.

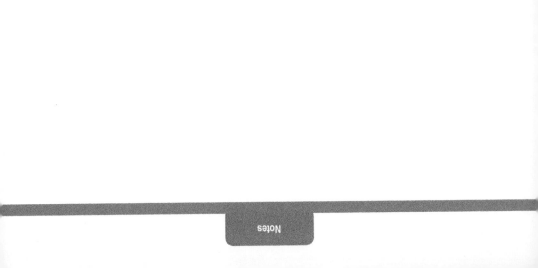

Notes

# 23: Introduction to consolidated financial statements

## Topic List

Overview

Definitions

Associates

*If a company has a subsidiary at its year end, it must **prepare group accounts** known as consolidated financial statements.*

## Basic principles

1. Consolidation means **adding together.**

2. Consolidation means **cancellation of like items** internal to the group.

3. Consolidate as if you **owned everything** then **show the extent to which you do not own everything.**

**Consolidation** means presenting the results, assets and liabilities of a group of companies as if they were **one** company.

| Overview | Definitions | Associates |
| --- | --- | --- |

## A subsidiary is an entity over which the parent has control

- Control is presumed to exist when the parent owns > 50% of the voting power (eg voting equity shares). Even when parent owns < 50%, it is still possible for control to exist.
- Parent has power to govern the financial and operating policies of the entity by statute or an agreement.
- Parent has power to appoint or remove a majority of members of the board of directors.
- Parent has power to cast a majority of votes at meetings of the board of directors.
- Parent has power over > 50% voting rights by agreement with other investors.

## Further definitions per IFRS 10 Consolidated financial statements

| | |
|---|---|
| **Control** | An investor controls an investee when the investor is exposed, or has rights, to variable returns from its involvement with the investee and has the ability to affect those returns through its power over the investee |
| **Subsidiary** | An entity that is controlled by another entity (known as the parent) |
| **Parent** | An entity that controls one or more entities |
| **Group** | A parent and its subsidiaries |
| **Non-controlling interest** | The equity in a subsidiary not attributable, directly or indirectly to a parent |

**Associate:** An entity over which the investor has significant influence.

**Significant** 
**influence:**
- The power to participate, but not to control.
- Assumed if hold > 20% of voting rights.

Associates are accounted for in consolidated accounts using the **equity method**.

## SOFP

**Investment in associate:**

| | |
|---|---|
| Cost of investment | X |
| Share of retained earnings/losses | X |
| Include in assets | X |

## Statement of profit or loss

Show group share of associate's PAT **before** group profit before tax.

# 24: The consolidated statement of financial position

## Topic List

Cancellation and part-cancellation

Goodwill

Non-controlling interests

Intra-group trading

*This chapter introduces the basic techniques you will need to prepare a consolidated statement of financial position.*

## Cancellation

When preparing a simple consolidated statement of financial position:

- Take the individual accounts of the parent company and the subsidiary and cancel out items which appear as an asset in one company and a liability in another.

- Add together all the uncancelled assets and liabilities throughout the group.

## Part cancellation

An item may appear at differing amounts in the parent's and subsidiary's balance sheets.

- The subsidiary's shares may have been acquired at a price other than nominal value, raising the issue of goodwill.

- The parent may not have acquired all of the shares of the subsidiary, raising the issue of non-controlling interests.

## Goodwill

Goodwill arises when the parent pays more for their investment than the fair value of the net assets they acquire.

Any preacquisition reserves of a subsidiary company are not aggregated with the parent company's reserves in the consolidated statement of financial position.

Goodwill is recognised as an **intangible asset** in the consolidated SOFP.

### Goodwill working

|  | $ | $ |
|---|---|---|
| Fair value of consideration transferred |  | X |
| Fair value of NCI at aquisition |  | X |
| Less net acquisition-date fair value of indentifiable assets acquired and liabilities assumed: |  |  |
| Ordinary share capital | X |  |
| Share premium | X |  |
| Retained earnings at acquisition | X |  |
| Fair value adjustments at acquisition | X |  |
|  |  | (X) |
| Goodwill |  | X |

## Non-controlling interest

Shows the extent to which net assets controlled by the group are owned by parties other than the parent.

## SOFP – equity

|  | $ |
| --- | --- |
| Fair value of NCI at acq'n | X |
| Plus NCI's share of post acq'n ret'd earnings | X |
| NCI at reporting date | X |

## Retained earnings

|  | PCo $ | SCo $ |
| --- | --- | --- |
| Per question | X | X |
| Adjustments (unrealised profit attributable to PCo) | (X) | |
| Pre-acq'n ret'd earnings | | (X) |
|  | | Y |
|  | | |
| Group share of post-acq'n ret'd earnings S Co (Y × %) | X | |
| Group ret'd earnings | X | |

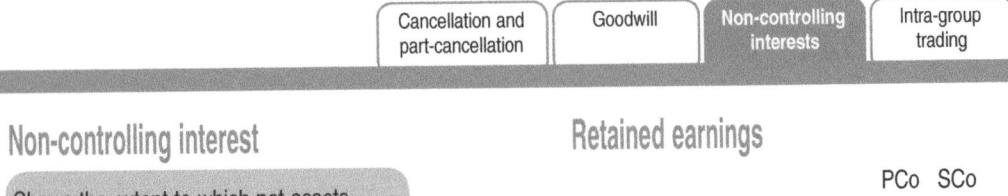

## Intra-group trading

Unrealised profit will arise on intra-group transactions where the inventory is still held at the reporting date:

1. Work out which company made the profit

2. Calculate the provision for unrealised profit (PUP)

3. For consolidation purposes, eliminate the profit from inventory and group retained earnings.

- If parent (P) sells to subsidiary (S), the unrealised profit lies in P's books:

  DEBIT Consolidated SPL (whole profit loading)
  CREDIT Group inventory

- If S sells to P, the unrealised profit lies in S's books and must be shared between P and the NCI:

  DEBIT Consolidated SPL (P's share)
  DEBIT Non-controlling interest (NCI's share)
  CREDIT Group inventory

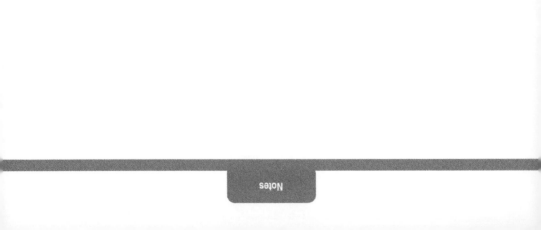

Notes

# 25: The consolidated statement of profit or loss

## Topic List

Consolidated statement of profit or loss

*Generally, the consolidated statement of profit or loss is more straightforward than the consolidated statement of financial position.*

Consolidated statement
of profit or loss

| | |
|---|---|
| Purpose | To show the results of the group for an accounting period as if it were a single entity. |
| Sales revenue to profit for year | 100% parent (P) + 100% subsidiary (S) (excluding adjustments for intra-group transactions). |
| Reason | To show the results of the group which were controlled by the parent company. |
| Intra-group sales | Strip out intra-group activity from both sales revenue and cost of sales. |
| Unrealised profit on intra-group sales | (a) Goods sold by P: increase cost of sales by unrealised profit.<br>(b) Goods sold by S: increase cost of sales by full amount of unrealised profit and decrease non-controlling interest by their share of unrealised profit. |
| Non-controlling interests | S's profit after tax $\qquad$ X<br>Less * unrealised profit $\qquad$ (X)<br>$\qquad$ $\overline{\text{X}}$<br>NCI% $\qquad$ $\dfrac{\text{X}}{\overline{\text{X}}}$<br><br>* Only applicable if sales of goods made by subsidiary. |

| Reason | To show the extent to which profits generated through P's control are in fact owned by other parties. |
|---|---|
| Acquisitions part way through the year | If a subsidiary is acquired during the year, only the post-acquisition element of the statement of profit or loss figures is included on consolidation. |

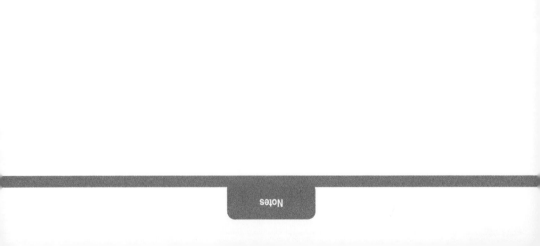

Notes

# 26: Interpretation of financial statements

## Topic List

*This section looks at how we can read and interpret the financial statements.*

*Ratios are a tool which allow us to assess the figures presented.*

Information required by users

Profitability and efficiency

Liquidity

Gearing

Limitations of ratio analysis

## Purpose

Analysis of a company's financial statements is performed by the following:

- Interested parties outside the business who are seeking to know more about the company (potential investors)
- Management wishing to interpret their company's past performance in order to make improvements for the future

As well as:

- Employees – will I get paid?
- Governments – tax, regulations compliance
- Suppliers/lenders – will we get paid?
- Customers – can we rely on this company?

Financial statements can be assessed using ratio analysis.

- Past trends of the same business (analysis through time) and compare to budget
- Comparative information for similar businesses (analysis by competitors)

# Return on capital employed

$$ROCE = \frac{PBIT}{Capital\ employed} = \frac{PBIT}{Total\ assets\ less\ current\ liabilities}$$

Measures overall efficiency of company in employing resources available to it.

Ways to use ROCE:

- Monitor changes in ROCE from year to year
- Comparison to similar entities
- Comparison with current market borrowing rates

Profit margin × Asset turnover = ROCE

# Return on equity

$$ROE = \frac{PAT\ and\ pref\ div}{Ord\ share\ capital + reserves}\ \%$$

More restricted view of capital than ROCE, but same principles.

# Profit margin

$$Profit\ margin = \frac{PBIT}{Sales}\ \%$$

$$Gross\ profit\ margin = \frac{Gross\ profit}{Sales}\ \%$$

Useful to compare profit margin (PBIT) to gross profit margin to investigate to movements which do not match.

# Asset turnover

$$Asset\ turnover = \frac{Sales}{Total\ assets\ less\ current\ liabilities}$$

Measures efficiency of use of assets.

## Current ratio

$$\text{Current ratio} = \frac{\text{Current assets}}{\text{Current liabilities}}$$

Should expect current ratio to be comfortably >1, but will depend on industry.

## Quick ratio

$$\text{Quick ratio (acid test)} = \frac{\text{Current assets} - \text{Inventory}}{\text{Current liabilities}}$$

- Eliminates illiquid and subjectively valued inventory.
- Could be high if overtrading with receivables, but no cash.
- Typically, should be at least 1; but could be lower in industries with fast inventory turnover (eg supermarkets)

## A/cs receivable collection period

$$\frac{\text{Trade receivables}}{\text{Credit sales}} \times 365$$

Consistent with normal credit terms? If not, investigate.

## Inventory turnover period

$$\text{Inventory turnover period} = \frac{\text{Inventory}}{\text{Cost of sales}} \times 365$$

Generally, the higher the better, but remember:

- Lead times
- Seasonal fluctuations in orders
- Alternative uses of warehouse space
- Bulk buying discounts
- Likelihood of inventory perishing or becoming obsolete

## A/cs payable payment period

$$\frac{\text{Trade accounts payable}}{\text{Purchases}} \times 365$$

Use cost of sales if purchases not disclosed.

## Debt ratio

Debt ratio = $\dfrac{\text{Total debts}}{\text{Total assets}}$ %

(> 50% = high)

## Gearing

Gearing ratio = $\dfrac{\text{Total long term debt}}{\text{Shareholders' equity} + \text{Total long term debt}}$ %

## Interest cover

Interest cover = $\dfrac{\text{PBIT}}{\text{Interest charges}}$

- Company must generate enough profit to cover interest.
- Is 3+ safe? Consider relevance of profit vs cash.

## Limitations

The limitations of ratio analysis are as follows:

- Comparative information is not always available.
- The information used is sometimes out of date.
- Interpretation requires thought and analysis. Ratios should not be considered in isolation.
- The exercise is subjective, for example not all companies use the same accounting policies.
- Ratios are not defined in standard form.

Notes

Notes

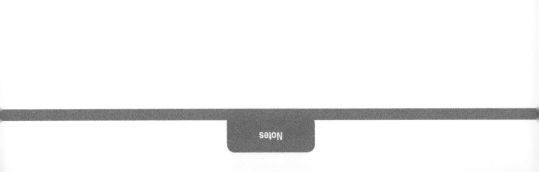

Notes

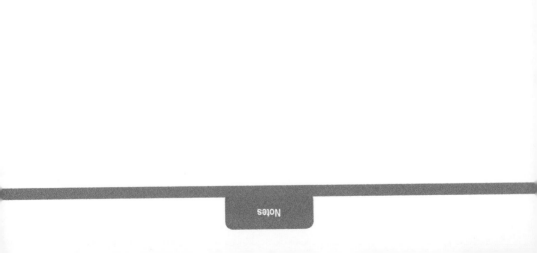

Notes

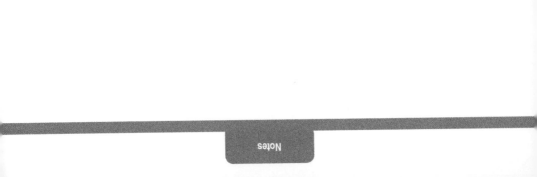
Notes

Notes